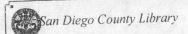
San Diego County Library

This book has been purchased for
the Poway Branch Library by the
Friends of the Poway Library
together with matching funds from
the San Diego County Board of
Supervisors.

SAN DIEGO COUN
W9-CGR-969
0621

WITHDRAWN FROM
SAN DIEGO COUNTY LIBRARY

Isaac Newton

Tony Allan

Heinemann Library
Chicago, Illinois

© 2001 Reed Educational & Professional Publishing
Published by Heinemann Library,
an imprint of Reed Educational & Professional Publishing,
Chicago, IL
Customer Service 888-454-2279

Visit our website at www.heinemannlibrary.com

All rights reserved. No part of this publication may be reproduced or transmitted in any
form or by any means, electronic or mechanical, including photocopying, recording,
taping, or any information storage and retrieval system, without permission in writing
from the publisher.

Illustrated by Michael Posen
Originated by Ambassador Litho
Printed in Hong Kong

05 04 03 02 01
10 9 8 7 6 5 4 3 2 1

Library of Congress Cataloging-in-Publication Data

Allan, Tony, 1967-
    Isaac Newton / Tony Allan.
        p. cm. -- (Groundbreakers)
    Includes bibliographical references and index.
    ISBN 1-58810-053-7
    1. Newton, Isaac, Sir, 1642-1727--Juvenile literature. 2. Physics--History--Juvenile
literature. 3. Physicists--Great Britain--Biography--Juvenile literature. [1. Newton, Isaac,
Sir, 1642-1727. 2. Scientists.] I. Title. II. Series.

    QC16.N7 A52 2001
    530'.092--dc21
    [B]
                                                                              00-063442

Acknowledgments
The author and publishers are grateful to the following for permission to reproduce
copyright material: AKG London, pp. 10, 13; Erich Lessing, pp. 17, 23,24,30, 33; Art Archive
7/Private Collection, p. 27; Bridgeman Art Library, p. 6; Lincolnshire County Council, Usher
Gallery, Lincoln, UK,, p. 25; Stapleton Collection, UK, p. 34; John Noott Galleries, Broadway,
Worcestershire, UK, p. 37; Corbis, p. 36; Mary Evans Picture Library, pp. 11, 16, 18, 28, 29,
31, 35, 43; MPM Images, pp 8, 12, 19, 41; By permission of the President and Council of the
Royal Society, pp. 9, 21, 39; Science and Society Picture Library, p. 4; Science Museum, pp.
14,20, 38; Science Photo Library, p. 5; Voler Steger/Peter Arnold Inc, p. 22; Sheila Terry, pp. 32,
40; Werner Forman Archive, p. 42.
Cover photograph reproduced with the permission of AKG London.

Every effort has been made to contact copyright holders of any material reproduced in
this book. Any omissions will be rectified in subsequent printings if notice is given to the
publisher.

Some words are shown in bold, **like this.** You can find out what they mean by looking in
the glossary.

Contents

Piecing Together the Universe

When Isaac Newton was born in England, in 1642, the world was changing fast. During the **Middle Ages,** the Church thought it had settled all questions about how nature worked. But by the seventeenth century, the modern age was dawning. Great thinkers such as the Italian inventor and mathematician Galileo and the French **philosopher** Descartes had led the way in searching for proof about how the world really worked, and new discoveries were being made all the time. It was the beginning of the **Scientific Revolution**—and Newton was to become its champion.

This champion of modern science came from humble beginnings. The son of a farmer who could not even sign his own name, Newton did not come from a learned family. He had a lonely and unremarkable childhood. But it was as a student at Cambridge University that Newton's real talent was recognized. At the age of 26, he became the university's youngest-ever professor of mathematics.

Sir Isaac Newton, age 60, was already a world-famous scientist when he posed for this portrait by Sir Godfrey Kneller in 1702, wearing a full-length wig.

Newton was born during a time of amazing scientific discovery. The previous 150 years had been a period of exploration, in which seafarers had pioneered the way to previously unknown lands: the Americas, India, the East Indies, and Japan. Then, at the turn of the seventeenth century, came the age of science. Technological breakthroughs unveiled new wonders: the telescope opened up the heavens, and soon after, the microscope revealed previously unseen miniature worlds.

Trial by mathematics

Before Newton's time, science had been a branch of **philosophy.** Students solved problems by talking them over, or by referring to the teachings of ancient Greek thinkers, such as Aristotle or Plato. These teachings had become accepted, but there was no proof that they were correct. The world was buzzing with new ideas, but they did not yet fit together as a whole.

Newton combined his ideas on movement, **gravity,** and the way the universe works to make sense out of the confusion. He made it his life's work to tie the loose ends of the new science into a complete system—one that could be tested by experiments and backed up by mathematics.

Newton's method of careful observation and experimentation is the basis of science as we know it today. No wonder people came to see him as a new kind of hero—the explainer of the universe.

This early microscope was designed by the Dutch inventor Anton van Leeuwenhoek. To use it, people looked through a tiny round lens clamped between two brass plates. The specimen was placed on the pin at the top of the screw.

Woolsthorpe Manor in Lincolnshire was Isaac Newton's childhood home.

Isaac Newton was born on December 25, 1642, in Woolsthorpe, a small village in Lincolnshire, England. He was named for his father, a local landowner, but never met him, since he died three months before young Isaac was born.

Isaac was a weak and sickly baby who was not expected to live through the night. In fact, he survived, but the outlook still did not seem bright. He was the only child of a young widow who had no one to help her run the family estate at Woolsthorpe Manor. When Isaac was three years old, his mother, Hannah, remarried. It was a decision that affected Isaac for the rest of his life.

A lonely childhood

Hannah's new husband was a wealthy clergyman named Barnabas Smith. He was more than 30 years older than Hannah. He did not want to have his stepson living in his house. Barnabas insisted that Hannah should leave Isaac behind at Woolsthorpe when she moved into his house in a neighboring village. Hannah's mother moved to the farm to take care of Isaac, but that was little consolation. Young Isaac had been the sole focus of his mother's love and attention, but now found himself seemingly abandoned. Hannah and Barnabas Smith went on to have three children together—Mary, Benjamin, and Hannah. Isaac had little to do with the other children. In the eight years that her new marriage lasted, Isaac saw his mother only on visits.

A WARTIME CHILDHOOD

During Isaac's childhood, a **civil war** (1642–49) raged through England. **Royalist** supporters of King Charles I were fighting against **Parliamentarians** who wanted the king to rule only with Parliament's approval. The Parliamentarians finally won, beheading Charles in 1649. There are no records of which side the Newton family supported. Although there was no fighting in Woolsthorpe itself, some of the battles were fought only short distances away, and troops of soldiers probably passed through the village. It must have been an unsettling time for Isaac and his family.

This painting shows a battle during the civil war. Country life went on much as usual through the war years while the opposing armies clashed in battle.

The experience marked Isaac deeply. Throughout his life, he was solitary and secretive, unwilling to trust other people. Isaac bitterly resented his mother and stepfather. He was always sensitive, and he seems never to have forgotten or forgiven the injury done to him. Isaac's secrecy would come to cause him difficulties later in his life.

A Growing Mind

Young Isaac spent several years studying at this school in nearby Grantham.

Very little is known about Isaac's early education, although he probably learned to read and write at the village school. In 1655, twelve-year-old Isaac went to the grammar school in the town of Grantham, about six miles (ten kilometers) away. That was too far to walk each day, so Isaac went as a weekly boarder, and stayed in the town. He was found a room in the home of the local **apothecary,** or pharmacist, an educated man who owned books that Isaac was allowed to read. Isaac also got his first taste of chemistry from helping to mix medicines in the shop. He continued to be fascinated by the subject his whole life.

Making models

It may have been in Grantham that he found a book that was to change his life. It was called *The Mysteries of Nature and Art,* and it developed Isaac's understanding of mechanical devices, like levers, pulleys, and gears—knowledge that he would find very helpful later. The book contained detailed instructions for making mechanical models. Isaac was good with his hands, and he threw himself into model-making with a passion.

Isaac made kites with firecrackers tied to their tails, sundials, a cart big enough to sit in with a crank to turn the wheels, and a windmill with working parts.

A quiet student

At school, Isaac would have studied classical Latin and Greek, Bible studies, and some English grammar. At first, Isaac was a shy student, very much caught up in his own thoughts. But he made a few friends when a local bully picked on him; Isaac challenged him to a fight and won. His schoolwork also improved, and he became a top student. By the time Isaac was in his mid-teens, his teachers realized that he had the makings of a university scholar. But that was not what his mother had in mind for him. She needed Isaac to run the family estate. So at age sixteen, he was taken out of school and returned to Woolsthorpe to work on the farm.

Isaac Newton was twelve in 1655, the year he left home to attend the King's School in Grantham.

The move was a disaster. Isaac had never shown any interest in farm work—his mind was on his studies, and he often forgot his farm duties. When he was eighteen, Isaac must have been delighted when Hannah finally agreed to let him go back to school in Grantham to prepare to enter the university.

A Changing World

When Isaac left the farm in 1661, it was an exciting time to be starting a scientific career. The **civil war** was long over, and in 1660, the **monarchy** had been restored. The new king, Charles II, strongly supported new scientific studies, and in 1662, gave official backing to the **Royal Society,** a scholarly club that was to become a center of scientific knowledge.

New developments

There was much for the society to consider. The **Scientific Revolution** was taking place, and a flood of new discoveries in every area of knowledge was changing the way that people thought. In Italy, Galileo Galilei had built telescopes powerful enough to show sunspots and the moons circling the planet Jupiter. In Prague, Johannes Kepler had worked out precise mathematical formulas suggesting how planets move. There had been other breakthroughs, too. The thermometer and the **barometer** had been invented, while in math, **logarithms** had been devised. These are tables of figures that helped people to make complicated calculations. In medicine, the English doctor William Harvey had figured out how the heart pumps blood around the body.

Johannes Kepler analyzed the motion of the planets before the invention of the telescope.

Testing theories

Behind all these breakthroughs was a change in the way people thought about the world. People such as Galileo and French **philosopher** René Descartes had led the way in challenging accepted authority—not just the Church, but the Greek and Roman writers, too. They said that scientific knowledge must be established by tests, experiments and mathematical proof—not just reasoning. These were the ideas that stirred Isaac's imagination when he began at Cambridge University, and they were the foundations on which he built his entire career.

In the years before Newton's birth, Italian scientist Galileo Galilei had made groundbreaking discoveries using telescopes of his own making.

Ancient Greek thinkers such as Aristotle and Plato believed that the earth was the center of the universe. They thought that the moon and planets moved around the earth in perfect circles, fixed forever in spinning, transparent spheres of glass-like crystal. For nearly 2,000 years, no one challenged these ideas. Then, around the year 1600, a Dutch spectacle maker named Hans Lippershey invented the spyglass, which Galileo later developed into the telescope. Soon, astronomers could see craters on the moon, comets flashing through the skies, and previously unknown moons circling other planets. The heavens were not perfect and unchanging after all—the Greek thinkers had been wrong.

The Young Scholar

Cambridge was less than 60 miles (100 kilometers) from Woolsthorpe, but even that was a three-day journey on horseback in Isaac's day. When Isaac arrived in June 1661, he found a dirty, busy, and smelly town. The town had a population of about 8,000 people, while Woolsthorpe was a village with just a few farms. Cambridge must have seemed an amazing place to someone like Isaac who had never before been far from home.

Cambridge was one of only two universities in England at the time. Isaac's mother chose to send him as a **subsizar.** This meant that as well as studying, Isaac had to pay his way by waiting on tables and acting as a kind of servant to other students. Isaac's mother could have afforded to pay his fees, but she did not really want him to go to the university, and may have wanted him to work for his education.

Life at Cambridge

The result was that Isaac had a miserable first two years, with few friends. No doubt he felt humbled by his lowly position.

*Trinity **College** at Cambridge University was where Newton, age eighteen, enrolled as a student in 1661.*

He threw himself into his studies and into religion, and he even kept a journal in which he wrote down lists of his sins. But life for Isaac gradually improved. In his third year, he made friends with a fellow student named John Wickins, with whom he would live for more than twenty years. Like Isaac, Wickins had a passion for science, and they worked together on many experiments.

It was at Cambridge that Isaac discovered new ways of thinking. At first, he spent most of his time studying the Greek thinkers who still made up most of the official course of study. But in 1663, a change showed through in his notebooks, where he wrote detailed accounts of his thoughts and findings—in Latin, the accepted language of science at the time. While he respected the great classical philosophers, Isaac wanted proof. He listed his own ideas, based on his reading of new thinkers such as Francis Bacon, Galileo, and Descartes, under a series of scientific headings, like "Of the Sun, Stars, Planets, and Comets," and "Of Attraction Magnetical."

Objects that once belonged to Newton, including a gyroscope and a pair of compasses, adorn his desk at Trinity College, Cambridge.

In Newton's words:

"Plato is a friend, Aristotle is a friend, but truth is the best friend of all."

(From Newton's notebook, written in 1663)

In fact, Isaac was so interested in these new thoughts that he neglected his official studies. When he took his final exams, he did not do very well. He still managed to earn his bachelor of arts degree, however. In addition, Isaac's passion for this new learning had caught the attention of some of the college staff. More importantly, Isaac himself had discovered what he wanted to do with his life. He had found his career—as a scientist.

Experiments with Light

This scientist conducts an experiment with a prism. Prisms were the keys Newton used to unlock the secrets of light and color.

In 1664, as a third-year Cambridge University student, Isaac did his first serious scientific research. He had bought a **prism,** a block of clear glass with angled sides, from a stall at the annual Sturbridge Fair, held just outside the town. Like countless people before him, Isaac enjoyed viewing the rainbow of different colors that the prism produced when he held it up to the light. But he was not content just to admire it—he wanted to understand what he was seeing.

With Wickins' help, Isaac covered the windows of his college room so that only a pinpoint of light could be seen. Then he placed the prism so that it cast a pattern of colored bands, known as the **spectrum,** on the opposite wall. Using other prisms, he carried out a series of experiments on the sun's rays.

Unpicking the rainbow

Isaac wanted to know why the light on the wall did not appear as a white circle, like the shape of the sun, but instead appeared as a series of colored bands. He quickly realized that it did so because sunlight, or white light, was made up of light rays of different colors. As they passed through the prism, the rays were bent slightly, or **refracted,** by different amounts, so that the separate colors could be seen.

Now that he knew how the prism broke the sun's rays into the colors of the spectrum, Isaac's next step was to see if the separate colors could be broken up themselves. So he set up a second prism in such a way that only the red band passed through it. But this band simply stayed red—and each of the other colors he tested also stayed the same color. The conclusion was obvious to Isaac: the white light of the sun was a different kind of light from the other colors, because it was a mixture of all of them.

ONGOING IMPACT) Seeing stars

Isaac's work on the spectrum had an impact on the development of **spectroscopy,** which has proved vital in modern astronomy. By studying the spectra, or bands of color, created by starlight, researchers can gather vital information about the temperature and chemical composition of distant stars, and even about the speed at which they are moving and the strength of their magnetic fields.

Isaac was fascinated by light and went on to make many more discoveries in the field that he called "Opticks." However, Isaac was not ready to share his findings. He had been secretive and distrustful ever since his lonely childhood—so the world had to wait for 40 years before he published his discoveries on the subject.

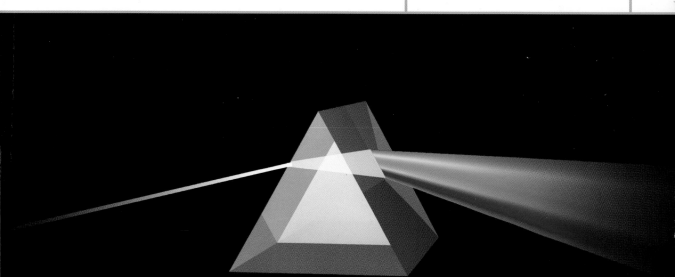

A prism separates light into the colors of the spectrum.

"Miracle Years"

When Isaac finished his university courses in 1665, the **plague** was sweeping through London. It soon spread to Cambridge, too. Fearing an outbreak, the university authorities closed the school. Isaac had no choice but to return to Woolsthorpe and wait for the university to open again.

Undertakers' men collect the body of a plague victim who has fallen dead in a London street.

Back home, Isaac's mother had found other people to manage the farm, so his help was not needed. Instead, Isaac found himself with lots of ideas and plenty of time on his hands. He did not waste a moment. He stayed up until all hours studying, writing, and making calculations. Isaac had plenty to think about, because he already had the beginnings of many of his future discoveries in mind. There were his ideas about light to develop, and he was also doing groundbreaking mathematical work that would provide the testing ground for all his later theories.

THE PLAGUE

The plague was carried from rats to humans by fleas. The disease had spread throughout Europe. It reached England in 1665, hitting London first, where at its height it struck down 10,000 people a week. It then spread out across the country, claiming the lives of almost 100,000 victims before gradually disappearing in the course of 1666.

An apple and a stroke of genius

But Isaac's stay at Woolsthorpe is perhaps best remembered for an incident he described to friends many years later. While sitting in

Some of Isaac Newton's belongings are on display at Woolsthorpe Manor, which is now kept open to the public as a monument to the scientist.

the orchard one autumn day thinking about the movement of the moon and planets, Isaac happened to see an apple fall from one of the trees. In a moment of inspiration, it occurred to him that the force pulling the fruit to the ground might be the same one holding the planets in their courses, keeping them from flying off into deep space.

What came to Isaac that day was no more than the germ of an idea—far from a fully-formed theory. It would take him many years to work out the details of what that moment of insight meant. But from that day on, the seeds of the law of **gravity** were planted in his mind. That was the true measure of his genius—to let an insignificant event in a country garden set in motion a chain of thought that would end up unlocking one of the fundamental laws of the universe.

Discovering Gravity

Newton watches an apple fall in the orchard at Woolsthorpe. Newton told friends that the sight helped to spark his discovery of the force of gravity.

For Isaac, the falling apple triggered the idea that the planet Earth exerts an invisible force on all objects. This force not only pulls an apple down to the surface and holds our feet there, it also reaches far into space and pulls on the moon. The moon's speed of movement means that it tries to go in a straight line, flying away from Earth into deep space. But the earth exerts a force that continually pulls on the moon, to hold it back and make it move in a curve. It is almost as if the earth is twirling the moon around on a piece of string. With these forces in balance, the moon travels endlessly around the earth.

The idea of gravity

The pulling force exerted by Earth is called **gravity,** or the gravitational force. Isaac quickly saw that gravity must be a feature of all objects, making them pull on, or attract, all other objects. Big objects have greater gravitational force than small ones. Also, the gravitational force of an object fades rapidly with the distance from it. Even your own body has a gravitational force, but it is too small for you to notice. The earth's gravity is much stronger, pulling you down to the ground and keeping the moon in orbit. The sun is so huge that its massive gravity keeps all the planets traveling in orbit around it.

This space shuttle in orbit is circling the earth at 17,500 mph (28,000 kph).

GRAVITY

Objects circling the Earth—from the moon to spacecraft in orbit, as shown here—are traveling at great speeds. They should fly off in a straight line into outer space. But they do not, and Newton realized that this could only be because another force was pulling them back towards the earth's center. He called this force gravity, and he saw it at work not just in the heavens but on Earth, too, pulling apples to the ground from tree branches.

The law of gravitation

Isaac worked on and off over the next twenty years on incredibly complicated calculations to prove his theory. The result was his law of universal gravitation. This linked together an object's weight (or mass), distance, and gravitational force in a simple mathematical formula, and it was one of science's greatest achievements. Newton's fundamental breakthrough made sense of the mysteries of planetary motion—and at last put to rest the ancient Greek vision of how the universe worked.

A Mathematical Breakthrough

Gottfried von Leibniz, a brilliant German mathematician, challenged Newton's claim to have invented calculus.

To test his theories, Isaac relied on mathematics. He had already realized that the accepted math of the day was barely up to the task. But he also knew that he could count on the help of a secret weapon. Even though it was just two years since he had started to study mathematics seriously, Isaac had already taught himself all there was to know at the time—and then had gone a step further. While still at Cambridge, before the **plague** struck, Isaac had begun to develop a new mathematical system of his own that he called fluxions. Today we know it as **calculus.**

ONGOING IMPACT Calculus

Newton's own system of math, called calculus, deals with situations where things continuously vary—for example, the speed of a car during a race. Using calculus, you can work out how fast the car is going, and how much it is speeding up and slowing down, for each minute, second, and even instant of travel—in no time at all. In general science, it is probably the most widely used type of mathematics today.

Keeping the secret

Most young scholars would have wanted to tell the world about such an important discovery, but Isaac preferred to keep it a secret. He used calculus to carry out the hugely complicated mathematics that the study of **gravity** required. Yet when he published his findings in 1687, Newton chose to write out his evidence in conventional math rather than reveal how he had actually worked them out.

Returning to Cambridge

In 1667, after the threat of the plague had passed, Cambridge University reopened, and Isaac was able to return. There his work caught the eye of Isaac Barrow, professor of mathematics at Trinity **College,** who soon realized that Isaac had made important discoveries. To persuade him to make them public, Barrow showed Isaac a recently published work by a Danish mathematician who was also doing pioneering work on calculus.

Horrified to think that someone else might take the credit for his invention, Isaac agreed to let Barrow show a paper he had written to a few selected scholars, including the president of the **Royal Society** in London. The paper was enough to establish Isaac Newton's reputation as a rising talent. But still he would not agree to have the work published. Newton's secretiveness caused him problems later in life, when disagreements about who had invented calculus involved him in some bitter arguments.

Arundel House was home to the Royal Society in 1667. Newton later helped to raise the money to buy a new building in Crane Court, London.

The Young Professor

By the time he circulated his paper on **calculus,** Isaac had won a **fellowship** at Trinity **College,** Cambridge. This allowed him to continue his research, and it also guaranteed him a tiny salary and a room in the college for life, in return for a few teaching duties.

On the strength of this success, Newton allowed himself one or two small luxuries and distractions. He had the rooms he shared with his friend John Wickins repainted, bought new clothes and furniture, and even briefly took up lawn bowling.

The Lucasian professorship

Newton soon gave up such distractions, though, to get back to serious science. To succeed in the academic world, he needed the support of older scholars. Isaac Barrow was one important ally. He was the first Lucasian professor of mathematics. This new post was created in 1663 and named after Henry Lucas, the college member who had provided the money for it when he died. The Lucasian professorship still exists today, and the present holder is another famous scientist, physicist Stephen Hawking. Newton became Barrow's assistant. Besides doing his best to encourage Newton to publish his work, Barrow also paid him to check over his own lectures for publication.

Newton was a Cambridge professor when this engraving was made.

As a professor at Cambridge at the time, Newton did not have very much to do. He had to give about twenty lectures a year, and had to make himself available to students for a few hours each week. In fact, he was not a good teacher, and many of his lectures were delivered to empty or nearly empty halls. Often, he cut them down from the hour he was allowed to 30 or even 15 minutes. Newton preferred to save his energies for his research, which soon won him such fame that the college authorities were happy to allow him to work as he wanted.

The library at Trinity College was built while Newton was a professor there. He gave money toward the building costs.

Barrow greatly admired Isaac Newton as a mathematician. So when Barrow decided to leave Cambridge for London in 1669, he did not hesitate to recommend Newton as his successor. The university authorities took his advice, and on October 29, 1669, Newton was appointed the second Lucasian professor. At the age of 26, he became the university's youngest-ever mathematics professor. It was quite a step for someone who had barely passed his exams for graduation just four years earlier!

The Sorcerer's Apprentice

Alchemists, like this one, believed that by studying, experimenting, and living blameless lives, they could find the secret of turning base metals into gold.

With his future at Cambridge guaranteed, Newton was free to follow his own interests. He soon found a new passion—chemistry. At the time, chemistry was still closely linked to the age-old, semimagical study of **alchemy.** Alchemists believed that, through experiments and meditation, they could eventually find the philosopher's stone, a magic substance that had the power to change inexpensive, or base, metals like lead into gold. Another goal for alchemists was to find the elixir of life, a medicine that could keep people young forever.

Many people today are amazed that a genius like Isaac would have become involved in what is now seen as a fake science. But at the time, it seemed there might be important secrets to be discovered. Some alchemists had made great discoveries in chemistry in the course of their research. There was also a secret-society side to alchemy that may have appealed to Newton, who always saw himself as a seeker of hidden knowledge.

The science of religion

Isaac Newton had other unusual interests. He had always been deeply religious, and felt certain that there were secret meanings to be found in the Bible. Newton's ideas almost got him into trouble with the Church, because he became convinced that Jesus had been created by God rather than being a part of God's essence—an idea that the Church had long considered a **heresy.**

This could have lost Newton his place at Cambridge, since as a **fellow** of Trinity **College** at the time, he was supposed to become a minister eventually. This was something his unorthodox beliefs would not allow him to do. Fortunately, in 1675, he got permission from King Charles II, an enthusiastic follower of the new science, not to fulfill this requirement.

Newton's Bible studies led him in some strange directions. He wrote books seeking to spell out God's plans for the future of the world from the words of the prophets and the Book of Revelation. He became convinced that there were hidden meanings in the layout of Solomon's temple in Jerusalem, as described in the Book of Ezekiel, and spent years trying to work out what they were. Although this research led nowhere, Newton continued to work on his theories right up to his death. They now seem to many people to have been a waste of time, but to Newton, they were just as important as his work on **gravity** or light.

This is an artist's impression of Solomon's temple in Jerusalem. Newton sought hidden meanings in its design.

Newton's Telescope

In a refracting telescope, light rays move in a single direction down the tube toward the viewer. In a reflector like the one Newton designed, the rays bounce back from a mirror at the end of the tube to a second mirror angled toward the eyepiece.

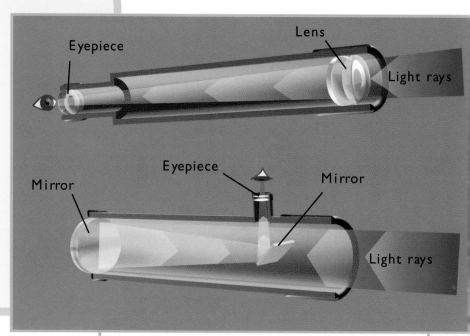

This shows a refracting (above) and a reflecting (below) telescope. Newton's reflecting telescope gave a clear picture and was easy to use.

Newton had other things besides **alchemy** on his mind in the late 1660s. He had not lost his talent for making things, and now he put it to use as an inventor. Newton designed and built a new kind of telescope, one whose basic principle is still in use in most of the world's great **observatories** today.

Early telescopes

The first telescope had been made in the Netherlands 60 years earlier by an instrument maker named Hans Lippershey. He had come up with the idea of placing lenses at both ends of a tube: one to collect light rays and focus them on to the other, an eyepiece that magnified them, at the far end. These first telescopes, called **refracting** telescopes because they bent, or refracted, the light, were crude devices. Galileo and other astronomers soon improved them, but they still made the images of stars fuzzy by surrounding them with a rainbow halo of colors.

Reflecting telescopes

Newton's solution was to use mirrors. These produced less distortion than lenses. His telescope had a curved, or **concave,** mirror at the back. This bounced the light rays forward to a second, smaller mirror halfway up the tube. The second mirror, in turn, reflected the light to an eyepiece, placed at the side of the tube rather than at its end.

In Newton's words:

"If I have seen further than most men, it is by standing on the shoulders of giants."

Newton was saying that had it not been for other great thinkers and scientists, including Descartes, Galileo, and Robert Hooke, he would not have been able to make so much progress himself.

(From a letter to Robert Hooke, who was a rival later on in Newton's life)

The idea of using mirrors instead of lenses was not new. It had been suggested several years earlier in a book called *Optica Promota* by a Scottish mathematician James Gregory, but no one had managed to make it work. Newton succeeded by doing everything himself. He produced his own design, made his own tools, and even ground his own mirrors and lenses. The results were even better than he could have imagined. The first reflecting telescope Isaac made magnified objects 40 times more than a much larger refracting telescope could manage.

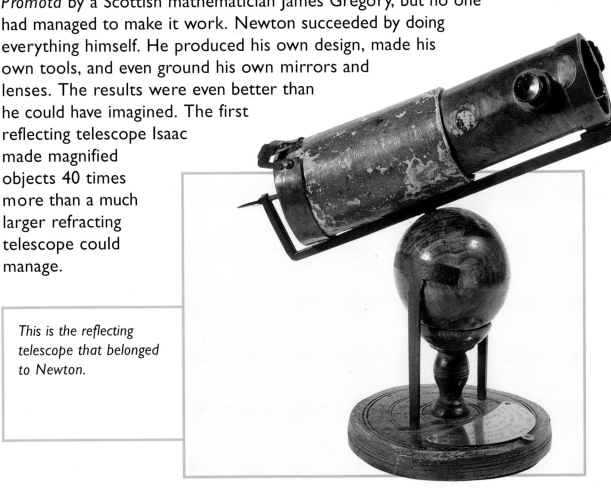

This is the reflecting telescope that belonged to Newton.

The Royal Society

SERIOUS SCIENCE?

Although the Royal Society was already highly thought of when Newton joined, it was also involved with a lot of matters that would not now count as serious science. In those early days, its members studiously listened to papers on such unlikely subjects as werewolves and ghostly spirits, as well as on weighty questions of astronomy, physics, and chemistry.

Many of Isaac Newton's theories were difficult for most people at the time to understand, but everyone could admire the reflecting telescope. It was Newton's ticket to success. When Isaac Barrow showed the new telescope to members of the **Royal Society** in London in December 1671, it caused a sensation—King Charles II himself was given a personal demonstration. As for Newton, he was honored with an invitation to join the society. The society's existing members, called **fellows,** included such celebrities as chemist Robert Boyle; Samuel Pepys, who was to write a famous diary of life in 1660s London; and Christopher Wren, who designed many buildings, including St. Paul's Cathedral in London.

At the society's meetings, papers describing new research were read and discussed. Soon after he became a Fellow, Newton sent a description of his work on light and color to a meeting of the society. Although he was not there to read it in person, it was a great success.

Samuel Pepys, author of a famous diary of seventeenth-century London life, was a member of the Royal Society in Newton's day.

This was a meeting of the Royal Society. Newton joined in 1672, and became its president in November 1703.

The price of fame

Not yet 30 years old, Newton had by now made his name. As a Cambridge professor and a fellow of the Royal Society, he was a rising star of English science. It was a fantastic advance for a young man who was totally unknown when he returned to the university after the **plague** just five years earlier.

But Newton's new fame came at a price. By publishing his findings for other scientists to study, he was also forced to explain and defend them. Newton was a very private man who had little patience when other, less learned men questioned his results. At such times, he would hurry back to Cambridge to lick his wounds, seeking the comfort of his **alchemical** research.

In Newton's words:

"I keep the subject constantly before me, till the first dawnings open slowly, by little and little, into the full and clear light."

(Isaac Newton, when asked how he made his great discoveries)

Quarrels

Most of Newton's troubles at the **Royal Society** stemmed from one person: Robert Hooke. Like Newton, Hooke was a talented young scientist, but unlike Newton, he was also very ambitious. Hooke was jealous of Newton's success, and soon tried to belittle his achievements.

Newton and Hooke first disagreed over Newton's paper on light. Hooke had been appointed **curator** of experiments by the society, responsible for testing new ideas. But he had his own ideas about light and color, and he dismissed Newton's theory without bothering to check it. Worse still, he claimed to have beaten Newton to the invention of the reflecting telescope, insisting that he had produced a similar instrument before the **plague** struck, though he had not kept it to prove his case.

This seventeenth-century engraving shows Robert Hooke carrying out an experiment on light using a pinhole camera.

ROBERT HOOKE

As well as being Newton's rival, Robert Hooke (1635–1703) was also one of the most talented scientists of his day. He did pioneering work in physics that helped pave the way for the invention of the steam engine. As an inventor, he devised improved versions of the microscope and the quadrant, an instrument used for pinpointing stars in the heavens. He was also an architect, and helped to draw up plans for rebuilding London after the Great Fire in 1666.

Rising anger

Newton was furious. Even at the best of times, he was hesitant to publish his discoveries. To have them challenged by someone he considered scientifically less than his equal seemed to confirm his worst fears about being misunderstood. Newton did not have the patience to argue his position, so instead he returned to Cambridge and sulked, even threatening to quit the Royal Society altogether. The dispute continued to simmer until Hooke's death in 1703.

The main effect of the quarrel was to drive Newton deeper into his **alchemy** studies at his laboratory in the gardens of Trinity **College.** He would stay up for much of the night, rarely going to bed before 3 A.M., so he could work on his alchemical experiments. Then, one day in the winter of 1677, he suffered a tragic loss when a candle started a fire on his desk while he was out of the room, burning some irreplaceable manuscripts. Newton was devastated.

Newton received more bad news when his mother died in 1679. He returned to Woolsthorpe to settle the estate. But his scientific studies had to wait. Many of his most important discoveries about **gravity** and motion remained unpublished, and might have stayed that way—to the world's loss—if it had not been for the encouragement of a new friend, Edmund Halley.

This engraving shows Newton discovering the fire that destroyed many of his papers in 1677. Some versions of the story claim his dog started the fire, but in fact there is no evidence that he had a pet.

Newton's Masterpiece

Newton's friend Edmund Halley was a fine scientist in his own right.

Edmund Halley was an astronomer who visited Cambridge to consult Newton about a question involving planetary orbits. Halley was astonished to learn that Newton had already worked out the solution years before, but had never published his research. Realizing that Newton might have other important secrets to reveal, Halley spent months gently coaxing him to put all his findings down in print.

Principia

Finally, Halley's encouragement paid off. Once he took up the challenge, Newton threw himself into explaining his discoveries. He worked long hours on the manuscript, often going without meals, and sometimes staying up through the night. The result, written in Latin, was his masterpiece. *Philosophiae Naturalis Principia Mathematica* (Mathematical Principles of Natural Philosophy), often known simply as *Principia*, was finally published at the **Royal Society's** expense in 1687. It was a book that was to change the course of scientific study.

In Newton's words:

"In the preceding books I have laid down the principles of philosophy; principles not philosophical but mathematical. It remains that, from the same principles, I now demonstrate the frame of the system of the world."

(From *Principia*)

The long-term importance of *Principia* became clear only in later years, when future generations put the ideas it contained to use. Over the years, Newton's discoveries inspired inventors and engineers to devise machines and engines, clocks and measuring devices, and eventually even trains and cars and spacecraft. Newton's ideas really worked, and many of the inventions that now make up our modern world would never have seen the light of day without his insights.

Principia summed up all Newton's work in the fields of **gravity** and motion over the previous twenty years. It described in detail not just how objects moved on Earth, but also how the planets moved through space. Most importantly, the book provided a mathematical framework that could be used to test Newton's ideas. Scientists soon realized that Newton had made a breakthrough in the study of motion.

The laws of motion

In *Principia,* Newton spelled out his three laws of motion:

1. An object will stay at rest or will continue to move in a straight line at a constant speed unless some force acts on it.

2. When a force acts on a moving object, the object will accelerate in the direction of the force at a rate that depends on its mass and on the size of the force.

3. Every action has an equal and opposite **reaction.** For example, when you let air out of a balloon's neck, the air rushing backward pushes the balloon forward.

PHILOSOPHIÆ
NATURALIS
PRINCIPIA
MATHEMATICA.

Autore *JS. NEWTON,* Trin. Coll. Cantab. Soc. Matheseos Professore *Lucasiano,* & Societatis Regalis Sodali.

IMPRIMATUR·
S. PEPYS, *Reg. Soc.* PRÆSES.
Julii 5. 1686.

LONDINI,
Jussu *Societatis Regiæ* ac Typis *Josephi Streater.* Prostant Venales apud *Sam. Smith* ad insignia Principis *Walliæ* in Cœmiterio D. *Pauli,* aliosq; nonnullos Bibliopolas. *Anno* MDCLXXXVII.

This is the title page of the first edition of Principia. *Newton wrote his masterpiece in Latin, the language of science in his day.*

The Black Years

Principia should have been the high point of Newton's life, but instead it ushered in one of his worst periods. In his work, he threw himself back into his studies of **alchemy,** but they led nowhere. Any hopes he might have had of achieving breakthroughs in chemistry like those he had made in physics (what Newton still called natural philosophy) faded away. Newton was also lonely. He had never found it easy to make friends. His only close companion, John Wickins, moved out of Cambridge in 1684, leaving Isaac very much on his own.

This 1688 oil painting by Henry Glindoni shows William of Orange and his advisers in a council of war. Newton welcomed the arrival of William to become king of England. But his hopes of winning an official post from the new ruler were soon dashed.

Politics

With time on his hands, Newton got sidetracked into politics. In 1685, Newton's royal patron, Charles II, died and was replaced as king by his brother, James II. James tried to force Cambridge University to offer degrees to Catholics, who at that time were

denied them. Newton, who was passionately anti-Catholic, helped to organize opposition to the move. When James lost the throne in 1688 to the Protestant ruler William of Orange, Newton was pleased to have backed the winning side. For a few months, he hoped to gain an official position, but nothing ever came of it.

When William of Orange became king of England, Newton, who had never before held a public post, briefly sat in Parliament as the appointed member for Cambridge University. He took little part in debates. It is said that the only time Isaac ever spoke was to ask for a window to be closed one day when he found himself sitting in a draft.

Depression

Convinced that his career was going nowhere, Newton sank into a deep depression. The symptoms may have been made worse by the chemicals he breathed in regularly as he worked over his alchemist's furnaces. Recently, some researchers who have analyzed samples of Newton's hair have shown that it contained high quantities of poisonous lead and mercury.

In the seventeenth century, Newton served in England's Parliament twice as the member for Cambridge University.

Eventually, Newton snapped. In 1693, he suffered a nervous breakdown. Although he quickly recovered, the causes of his black mood did not go away. To fully regain his balance, he needed a new challenge, and in 1696, one came about in a most surprising way.

Master of the Mint

While Newton was at the Royal Mint, ridged edges were added to coins to deter **counterfeiters.**

The opportunity Newton had been waiting for finally came when he was least expecting it. Out of the blue, he was offered the job of **warden** of the Royal Mint, the organization responsible for making England's currency. Newton was delighted, even though it meant putting his scientific research aside and leaving Cambridge, where he had lived for the last 35 years. In 1696, at the age of 53, Newton set off for London and a new life.

An important job

The job at the mint was totally unlike anything Newton had done before, but it was an important one. The nation's money was under threat from forgers and "clippers," who trimmed the edges off coins for the valuable metal they contained, gradually reducing their real value. To beat the clippers, the government had decided to collect all the nation's money and replace it with newly minted coins with stamped edges.

NEWTON'S NIECE

When Isaac made the move to London, his seventeen-year-old niece, Catherine Barton, came from Lincolnshire to serve as his housekeeper. She was the only woman, apart from his mother, who ever shared Newton's home. Catherine was a bright, attractive girl, and she got to know many famous people through her uncle, winning the admiration of such celebrities as the writer Jonathan Swift, famous for his book, *Gulliver's Travels.*

Workers at the Royal Mint worked hard to produce new coins in Newton's day.

The battle for the coinage

Newton took his new responsibilities very seriously. He found ways to increase the efficiency of the mint, which was already working day and night to turn out the new money. He fiercely punished laziness and corruption among his staff. Newton even played detective to track down forgers and clippers, often going to prisons or slums to seek them out and to cross-examine them. Many of those he helped to catch were later hanged.

Increasing responsibilities

It was a very different life from the academic calm of Cambridge, but Newton loved it. He was now a wealthy man, with a coach to travel in, and a staff of about six servants. He loved the color red, and had red draperies and bed hangings and a red couch at his home. Newton took on new responsibilities, too. In 1700, he was promoted to become master of the mint, and in 1701, he reentered Parliament. Then, in 1703, shortly after the death of his old enemy, Robert Hooke, he was elected president of the **Royal Society.** The black years were long gone. Now he was an important public figure, respected even by people who knew nothing about science.

Newton's Last Years

In his last years, Newton found the fulfillment that he had wanted for so long. In 1704, a year after the death of his old enemy, Hooke, Newton published *Opticks*. Written in English to reach a wider audience, *Opticks* summed up Isaac's work on light over the past 40 years. The book was received with universal admiration, and it confirmed Isaac's position at the forefront of science. Across Europe, he was by now seen as one of the great men of his time.

A great honor

As president of the **Royal Society,** Newton ruled almost like a dictator over the English scientific world, arranging for members who lost his favor to be expelled. He had a group of young followers who hung on his every word, regarding him as the guiding genius of the age. Newton was honored outside scientific circles, too. In 1705, he was knighted to become Sir Isaac Newton—the first scientist ever to receive the honor.

This illustration is from Opticks, *Newton's last great work. Unlike the earlier* Principia, *it was written in English so more people could understand it.*

THE FRENCH PROPHETS

Although he was a devout believer, Isaac Newton's religious views remained unusual. When a group of exiles from France known as the French Prophets began prophesying and having visions in public, rumor claimed that Isaac took an interest in their views. But he did nothing to help them when they were put on trial for disturbing the public order—even though one of the accused was a longtime friend.

This was Newton in his old age. He lived to be 84, and was universally recognized as a great man.

Newton remained fiercely protective of his reputation. When German scientist Gottfried von Leibniz published his version of **calculus,** Isaac bitterly accused him of stealing his ideas. He would not accept that any rival could have come up with the same answers without cheating.

After the publication of *Opticks,* Isaac did little new science, choosing to spend his time instead on studying ancient history and dating events in the Bible. He remained deeply religious, as he had been from his student days.

At last he had gained the recognition he had long felt was his due. When Newton died on March 20, 1727, at the age of 84, he was buried in Westminster Abbey, the resting place of England's kings. Two dukes, three earls, and the lord chancellor of England carried Newton's coffin to the grave—a mark of the enormous respect his work had earned him.

The New Science

Isaac Newton was a pioneer of modern scientific methods, in which theories have to be put to the test to check that they really work. To prove his own ideas, he relied mainly on math, which underpinned much of his research. That, in turn, was possible only because he had himself made revolutionary advances in the subject—progress that might have been even more influential if he had been less sensitive about revealing his secrets to the world at large.

But the importance of Newton's work went beyond science alone. Before his day, the new discoveries made by the pioneers of the **Scientific Revolution** had challenged old ideas without offering a new world view to put in their place. What Newton offered was a whole new system to explain the working of the universe—and one that could be understood by human reason.

The Grand Orrery
And all other Mathematical Instruments made and sold by
—— BENJA^N. COLE, ——
at y^e Royal Exchange. or at his House in Ball-Alley going out of George-Yard, into Lombard Street.

*An instrument maker advertises an orrery, or mechanical model of the **solar system**. Demand for such devices rose in Newton's day.*

This is the inner solar system as we know it today. Newton's work was crucial in showing how the planets stay in their courses.

Newton's work on **gravity** had made him the first person in history to understand the way in which the earth moves through space, and to explain the motions of the planets. Then he had gone on to show that—amazingly—the forces shifting the heavenly bodies were at work much closer to home, in the moon's orbit and even in the fall of a simple apple. This meant that the same principles applied on Earth and in space—a single theory to explain the whole universe.

His discoveries may have been cosmic in scale, but they also had down-to-earth applications. His work inspired countless inventions that between them opened the way for the Industrial Revolution, and thus for the modern world.

The effect on the way in which people saw the world was just as far-reaching. Isaac Newton's universe seemed itself to work like a machine, one controlled by unbreakable rules. For Newton, a religious man, these laws had been established at the beginning of time by God—but God had framed them in a way that the human mind could understand. Reason, it seemed, ruled over all.

Newton's Legacy

For 250 years, Isaac Newton's model of the universe reigned supreme, ushering in a new age of progress. His laws worked very well for describing how things move on Earth and in our own **solar system**—the universe Newton himself had known. Much of the modern world, from space rockets to satellite TV, could never have come into being without Newton's discoveries.

But with time, knowledge moved on. In the centuries after Newton's death, new generations of scientists used better telescopes to learn more about outer space than Newton could ever have dreamed. Then, later still, improved microscopes uncovered another new world, dealing with the very, very small—the world of atoms. In these areas of unimaginably distant galaxies and of tiny atomic particles, new theories were needed to explain everything that came to light.

Newton is buried in Westminster Abbey, the resting place of England's kings.

In Newton's words:

"I do not know what I may appear to the world, but to myself, I seem to have been only like a boy, playing on the seashore, and diverting myself in now and then finding a smoother pebble or a prettier shell than ordinary, while the great ocean of truth lay all undiscovered before me."

(From Joseph Spence's *Anecdotes, Observations, and Characters of Books and Men Collected from the Conversations of Mr. Pope and Other Eminent Persons of His Time,* 1820)

Albert Einstein was the first to seriously challenge Newton's view of how the universe works, but he always acknowledged his debt to the work of his great predecessor.

More than 200 years after Newton, another genius, Albert Einstein, put his mind to explaining these fresh puzzles. The picture of the universe he came up with was very different from Newton's. From the 1920s, Einstein's view of a **relativistic** universe, in which space could bend and mass could change, did not entirely replace Isaac's ideas, but it did extend them. The universe, it turned out, was more complicated than even Isaac Newton had imagined.

The many new pioneers of modern science could never have had their groundbreaking insights if Isaac Newton had not shown them the way. His ideas have never gone out of date. Engineers working on high-technology projects still put his discoveries to use every day, and his laws are still taught to every would-be physicist.

Although Newton was in many ways a difficult man—a loner and a tireless worker who never found it easy to open himself up to other people—no man ever put his time to better use. By following the problems that obsessed him, he did something only a handful of people in history have ever done: discovered a whole new way of explaining how the universe works.

Timeline

1642   Isaac Newton born on December 25, at Woolsthorpe Manor, Lincolnshire, England. His father had died three months earlier.

1646   Hannah, his mother, marries Barnabas Smith, the rector (clergyman) of a neighboring village, and moves into his home.

1649   King Charles I is beheaded. England becomes a republic.

1653   Barnabas Smith dies. Isaac's mother returns to Woolsthorpe.

1655   Newton enters grammar school in Grantham.

1660   The monarchy is restored. Charles II becomes king of England.

1661   Newton enters Trinity **College,** Cambridge, as an undergraduate.

1665   Graduates with bachelor of arts degree. An epidemic of **plague** closes the Cambridge colleges, forcing him to return to Woolsthorpe.

1665–66   The "miracle years." Newton makes several vital breakthroughs in his scientific studies.

1667   Returns to Trinity College and is elected a **fellow.**

1669   Appointed Lucasian professor of Mathematics.

1671   Presents his reflecting telescope to the **Royal Society.**

1672   Elected a Fellow of the Royal Society.

1679   Death of Hannah, Newton's mother.

1682   Observes what will later be known as Halley's comet.

1684   Edmund Halley encourages Newton to publish his discoveries in the fields of **gravity** and motion.

1685   Death of Charles II. The pro-Catholic James II becomes king.

1687   Newton helps to oppose the offer of degrees to Catholics at Cambridge. Publishes his masterwork, *Mathematical Principles of Natural **Philosophy,*** written in Latin.

1688   James II is driven out of England.

1689   William of Orange becomes king. Newton is elected to Parliament as the member for Cambridge University.

1693   Newton suffers a nervous breakdown.

1696   Moves to London to become **warden** of the mint.

1700   Appointed master of the mint after the previous master's death.

1701   Elected to Parliament for the second time; holds the seat until 1705.

1703   Elected president of the Royal Society.

1704   Publishes *Opticks,* written in English to reach a wide audience.

1705   Knighted Sir Isaac Newton by Queen Anne.

1727   Newton dies on March 20 at the age of 84. He is given a state funeral and buried in London's Westminster Abbey.

More Books to Read

Anderson, Margaret J. *Isaac Newton: The Greatest Scientist of All Time*. Berkeley Heights, N.J.: Enslow Publishers, 1996.

Christianson, Gale E. *Isaac Newton and the Scientific Revolution*. New York: Oxford University Press, 1996.

McPherson, Joyce. *The Ocean of Truth: The Story of Sir Isaac Newton*. Lebanon, Tenn.: Greenleaf Press, 1997.

Glossary

alchemy early form of chemistry, the main goal of which was to find the secret of turning ordinary metals into gold

apothecary old term for a pharmacist

barometer instrument for measuring air pressure

calculus advanced mathematical technique, separately developed by Newton and by Gottfried von Leibniz in Germany, that can be used to measure areas, volumes, and rates of change

civil war war between citizens of the same country; in Britain, a war between Royalists and Parliamentarians, fought from 1642 to 1649

college part of a university

concave curving inward

counterfeiter forger; someone who produces fake money or other valuables

curator someone who has responsibility for looking after things

fellow member of certain public bodies. At universities, it may be the holder of a paid research post providing study facilities, usually in return for some teaching duties

gravity natural force, described by Newton, that attracts objects to one another

heresy going against the teachings of the Catholic Church

logarithm sequence of numbers, first worked out by the Scottish mathematician John Napier in 1614, that can be used to simplify the multiplication and division of large sums

Middle Ages period in European history between roughly A.D. 1000 and 1500, when the teachings of the Church dominated society and people's thinking

monarchy form of government with a king or a queen ruling a country

M.P. member of Parliament

observatory building where astronomers use telescopes to study space

Parliamentarian supporter of Oliver Cromwell during the British civil war; fought against Royalists

philosopher person who studies the history of ideas to create new ideas about truth and knowledge

philosophy use of reason and argument to seek truth and knowledge

plague lethal infectious disease marked by the development of swollen glands, especially in the armpit or groin

prism transparent object, usually with rectangular sides and triangular ends, that breaks up light into the colors of the spectrum

reaction in Newton's theory, the equal and opposite force acting on an object when it exerts force on another object

refract to bend

relativistic related to relativity, a concept developed by Albert Einstein to describe what happens to objects when they are traveling very fast, at or near the speed of light

Royalist supporter of the king during the British civil war; fought to keep the monarchy in Britain

Royal Society club set up in London in 1662 to promote research into the sciences

Scientific Revolution movement in the sixteenth and seventeenth centuries that produced new insights about how the world works by applying scientific techniques of observing, experimenting, and checking

solar system the sun and the planets that orbit it

spectroscopy scientific method based on analyzing the spectra given off by different light sources

spectrum colors into which white light breaks down when passed through a prism

subsizar in the seventeenth century, an undergraduate who had to earn his way through college by performing menial tasks

warden officer in charge of something

Index